For my daughter, Nancy,
who makes good things happen

Acknowledgments

This book would not have been possible without the belief, hard work, encouragement and devotion of my husband, David.

My son John respected the time I set aside to write. He also contributed his insight and humor.

To Nancy. My gratitude forever.

Thank you Nikki Giglia, Lindy Gifford and Cheryl McKeary at Maine Authors Publishing who have been patient and cheerful guides during this adventure.

Susan Winslow, Roz Gerst, Tom Foley and Richard Herman have listened to and read my writings for years. They are never shy with helpful critique or praise. Susan and Roz have been with me from the beginning of this project, always steadfast and encouraging. I looked it up. Ways of saying 'thank you' seem to be limited, so I will tell you that I am thankful to you all from the bottom of my heart.

Dona Sherburne unknowingly titled this book. I am so pleased.

Remembrance with gratitude to Keith Sherburne, friend and instructor, who believed in my poetry and gave so much of himself to Senior College.

My thanks to Susan Morrow for many things, especially for featuring my poetry on the Olli Art Wall.

I am forever grateful to Pat Muzzy who encouraged me to submit 'Her Hands Were Always Busy' to the Maine Senior College Network poetry contest.

By establishing the Senior Players, Mel Howards gave many of us a place for our creative voices. Fulfillment and fun! I bow to you with thanks.

I acknowledge Denney Morton, Pat Budd, Bill Gregory and Eleanor Steele for teaching wonderful poetry classes.

Harriet Passerman quietly said 'book' to me for years. It is my joy to say, "Done!"

My parents, Ernest and Ida Spinney, who believed in possibilities, would have been thrilled with this book.

I am blessed.

Contents

Lemon-Drop Day

Have you ever had a wonderful day
To savor slowly, like a lemon drop, let's say?
Unwrapped at daybreak, promise in your palm,
A bright sunny orb suggesting pleasure, calm?
Taste it. Perky, crisp, just right sour-sweet
To alert all senses, aware to greet
Adventure and reverie, each in turn
With equal enthusiasm, eager to learn
Life's mysterious meanings, large and small,
Carefully stored for easy recall,
A shield against bitter wormwood,
Adversity's darkness over good.
If wishes are given along the way,
Grant me an occasional lemon-drop day.

Enough

Perhaps I listen too hard in cathedrals
For answers that elude me.
There is something in the air
In hallowed places where granite stones
Are worn uneven by shoes
Scraping away at layers of time.
Even in dim wintery sunlight
Tall windows tell ancient tales in rich color.
I hear the hush of figures
Reposing into wooden pews,
Heads bowed in prayer.
I listen for a breath at my ear
Whispering solutions to life's riddles.
Instead I find serenity in solitude
And know the heart's steady rhythm.

My bond is beyond sacred walls:
In a drop of rain, a newborn babe,
A flower's hue, the kindness of hand to hand.
I am gathered into Mother Nature's lap,
Comforted, at home, and hear the music
Of her symphony that becomes a lullaby.
That is enough. I am at peace.

Color

Little tubes of paint
Red, yellow, blue
Have strength
To tell a story, define a culture,
Capture history, sway opinion.

And there's gentle power
In those tubes
To blush a baby's cheek,
Gild a golden locket,
Create rainbows,
Lift the spirit,
Sing the soul.
Color.

To Ivan Moravec, Classical Pianist

With the hall hushed, lights dimmed, anticipation high,
You, who were unknown to me, stepped onto the stage and said,
"Please, may we have the house lights up tonight?"

Aha—

You touched the keys and aliveness happened.
Our vital connection was made.
Quiescent hopes and dreams,
Once new before dust-gathering days, stirred.

I forgot to breathe.

Dream weaver, tension builder, spellbinder
Casting enchantment note by note,
You created a magic musical elixir.
Smooth as silk the satin potion went down,
Filling me with light and joy.

When the music thundered and rolled,
I trusted you to lead me back to a melodic Eden.
As you did, I followed and there found peace.
It was an evening of wonderment.

I did not know I could hold my breath so long.

As Pooh Would Say

As my pal Winnie-the-Pooh would say,
"Let's have 'a little something' today."

Dip in the honey pot for a taste of grace.
A spoonful of forgiveness has its place

Between parent and child, husband and wife,
To lower the volume, ease the strife.

Soothe heartache with honey-balm
Of understanding, tolerance, calm.

Take a moment. Sit under a tree with me.
Dip into the honey pot of love and see

How much life-sweetness is there for you.
Take a moment to hear my pal Winnie-the-Pooh.

Louis Armstrong Leads the Parade

In the beginning,
a small boy in the Children's Home learned to read music,
picked up a military band's leftover cornet,
and pushed joy and love through a horn.

During the early days,
his long-time wife pounded out the beat,
flat-footed connection to terra firma,
one eye on Louie, one on the books,
while he poured out his soul and called it Jazz.

Then
he showed the Big Boys in the Big Bands
what could be. They came behind and with, never ahead,
making their own splendid music,
while Louie went universal.

Bright-eyed, satchel mouth, shiny trumpet, pristine handkerchief,
invented his scat and magical style,
took us up, up out there on a heartbreak high note,
gifted to us his Wonderful World. Amen.

Yea-a-a-a-a.

Waiting for Words

I am waiting.
Blank page.
A pencil
Imprinted with the word
"Inspire"
Waits with me
Poised above empty space.
My dozing muse
Speaks out of a dream.
"Be still and listen."

This is not a day
Words thump about
Demanding freedom
In paper and print,
Blaze across my mind-sky
To be captured
Or lost forever.

Rather, wonder, on tiptoes
Peeks around inner corners
To discover what is there:

A tear left over
From a sad goodbye,
A smile saved
To lift a cloud,
A prayer of hope,
The longing for peace,
Music, always music.
And laughter.

The pencil moves.
My muse smiles
In her slumber.

Metaphor, Anyone?

Apologies are afterthoughts for unkindness.
Bakeries are hotbeds of diet challenge.
Cookies are Band-Aids for minor cuts and bruises.
Delight is happiness with dancing feet.
Enough is a flashing stop sign.
Faith is a blindfolded walk along a cliff edge.
Grammar is the watchdog of proper communication.
Hobbies are gatekeepers to creativity.
Idleness is neutral gear for the brain and body.
Junkyards are grave sites for discarded dreams.
Kisses are silent love stories.
Luck is the life preserver in the sea of despair.
Mile markers are carrots in front of marathon runners.
Nutshells are baskets for pithy ideas.
Open windows are welcoming committees for spring breezes.
Punctuation is a tossed salad of dots and dashes.
Questions are first steps on the road to discovery.
Race horses are beauty in fast forward.
Staples are paper hangers.
Toothpaste is spearmint in whispered sweet nothings.
Umbrellas are portable insurance policies against bad hair days.
Violin solos are languages without words.
Windshield wipers are metronomes on rainy road trips.
X-rays are snoops that get under your skin.
Yawns are periods at the end of a busy day.
Zippers are the vengeful goddess Nemesis in my wardrobe.

Iced Tea

Come along with me to find a shady tree,
A leafy one with sunbeams dancing through
beneath puffy clouds drifting in the blue
summer sky where hawks wheel free.
We will have dainty cucumber sandwiches
And sparkling icy tea.
Come, my dear, my friend. Come with me.

Who Was She?

Did Whistler's mother ever sing
Or tap her toe to keep the beat,
Mark time, feel the music
Right down to her feet?

Did she hum a little
"Nearer My God to Thee,"
A bit of lullaby, a nursery rhyme
She learned at three?

Did a ringlet ever escape
To lie along her cheek?
Was there laughter in her voice
When she opened her mouth to speak?

Who was this woman, sitting so still?
How did she move through her life?
Did her boundaries go beyond
The sister, the maternal, the wife?

Straight and proper, silent in black,
A lovely picture by son of mother,
This is the side we see.
But I would rather know the other.

Last Day

He woke
He rose
He knelt
He prayed.

He lifted
He struggled
He staggered
He prayed.

He thirsted
He suffered
He bled
He prayed.

He wearied
He forgave
He exhaled.
Jesus died.

His Journey

In the beginning
The sun rose
With every promise
Dawn had to offer,

Dazzled bright
With midday possibilities.

Cooled.

Wandered into shadowy dusk.
Seduction beckoned
Beyond control.

Moon and star-shine gone,
Darkness deepened.

No more will the son rise.

Hearts break beyond repair,
Beyond love's power.
Only memory lingers.

Oh, my child, my child.

Bitter Fruit from the Tree of Hate

Two old women sit in the house on the hill,
At last sovereigns of all they survey,
Running their fingers through coin and jewel,
Eyes bright, lips twitch where covert smiles play.

The ancient dog is gone, geraniums wither and die.
Birds peck at near-empty feeders.
It is quiet and dim when shades are drawn
As shadowy forms come to read the meters.

Two old women sit in the house on the hill,
No cutting remark or vengeful retort is said.
The common bond, the lifelong object of their envy and hate,
The third old woman, their sister, is dead.

Heart Song Remembered

When I said,
"Come play your pan pipe for us,"
You paused not a moment
To ask, "Can I?"
Just lifted the magic
To your lips,
And with feet a-dancing,
Led us lightly
Through daisies and clover
While robins brunched
In the wild apple tree.

It was that June.

Fate

Fate has brought me
To the Font of Fear,
Dipped its fingers into the icy water,
Touched my forehead
And left its damp mark
Upon my heart for the rest of my days,
Nevermore to be free of that baptism.

Archers Have No Gender

You didn't stand before me,
appropriate paces apart,
Nor pin a painted bull's-eye
right above my heart.

You didn't take a solid stance,
slowly raise the weapon to your eye,
pull the string to bend the bow,
hold your breath—then let the missile fly.

There was no awful thwack
or crushing bone at lethal hit,
no telltale expression on your face
to make the puzzling pieces fit.

Oh, no. It was a gentle arrow,
making very little sound,
that swiftly honed in on me
until the vital mark was found.

It was the disapproving glance, a need ignored,
that sent the shaft into my soul.
Every hug held back, each irritated sigh,
nicked my heart, left a little hole.

They were such tiny wounds.
Perhaps you thought it never mattered,
but the love seeped out, drop by drop,
until at last all hope was shattered.

Me? Love again? To myself I say—
Beware. Do not be misled.
Remember how painful silent heartbreak can be.
Listen very well to what's unsaid.

Distant Farewells

Death came to us twice this week,
Distances from our door but deeply felt.

The first with such heartbreak.
We did not know the young man,
Son of caring mother and father,
Caught in the horror grip of addiction,
Restless inner demons
Driving him into unknown darkness,
Destroying any claim to this Earthly walk,
Joyous morning waking or peaceful heart.
Tears are for his parents' despair,
All hope and solace gone,
Condemned to know this death
To the end of their days.

The second, across the ocean.
Our friend waged a valiant battle
Against overwhelming odds.
His was truly a good life
Lived by a good man,
Husband, father, grandfather, teacher.
His death came with sorrow's grateful sigh.
His mountain was too steep.

We speak quietly of these deaths.
For what is to become of the people left behind
Who mourn their passing and love them still?

Too Soon

Oh, to write a poem so pretty or something witty,
Show the bright side, taking care to hide
My aching heart and tears that start
At recalling your face or something you said.
I bend my head to shade my eyes.
A smile is my disguise. I tell myself
My sorrow will keep until night is deep
And, seeing your image in the moon,
I whisper, "It's too soon—too soon."
I wanted to know you forever.

Her Hands Were Always Busy

Her hands were always busy.
Unadorned, save the slender silver ring,
Third finger, left hand, that changed her name,
Defined her as wife.

Suds to elbows, those hands lifted sheets to wringer.
Icy fingers pried frozen towels from the line.
Laundry was no push-button chore.

With clicking needles, she knit
Precious little white mittens
With dear pink angora bunnies on the backs
For the delicate-boned, red-haired girl cousin.
There were sturdy sliding, snowball-making
Mittens for the four boy cousins.
Babies and toddlers got colorful felt slippers
And feather-stitched flannel petticoats against winter's chill.

She could cane a chair, paint and paper, make Christmas wreaths.
Also wrote the village news for our local weeklies.
On Saturday afternoons she listened to radio opera
As she scrubbed the big kitchen floor.

What were her thoughts as she planted, weeded,
Hoed, picked, canned, whipped, stewed,
Arranged a home-grown birthday bouquet for her father
While his angel food cake baked golden in the oven?
Family and friends, expected or not,
Always had a place at her table.

I never saw my mother twiddle her thumbs.

The Beach

Eons of ice and storms made the beach grain by grain. Not very wide, it wedged
Between two brooding boulders that created boundaries. There toddlers and tykes
Played mornings away with pails and shovels.

After lunch, bigger kids swam, cannonballed off the rocks, made up water games,
Snorkeled. Sometimes they stood perfectly still in the crystal, clean lake water to watch
Minnows nibble at their toes.

Old pines cast late-afternoon shadows while two grandmothers lodged colorful
Webbed chairs into sand at water's edge, occasionally paddling their feet as they
Chatted.

At nightfall, sun-soaked and waterlogged, sleep beckoned all to the melody of a
Rowboat nudging gently against the wooden dock.

A Dad Story

We spoke in class about Wordsworth wandering his hill of daffodils,
Working silently in his soul during that seemingly indulgent stroll.

I flash back to the farm where I grew up. Chicken farm, that is—was.
Five thousand beasties demanding feed and routine, a job of
  never-ending chores.
My father was a good farmer.

One day we, a stair-step tribe of three, hatched a plan.
Do the work. Free up his time. After that make our request.
Maybe Dad would take us, as a rare treat, to see a longed-for movie.
The strategy seemed good.

What did he think when we rushed to carry water, weigh grain,
Spread corn, gather those eggs? Hot and sweaty, we finished our tasks.
Did he think we were growing up, suddenly kind and helpful?
  Unbidden?
Probably not. He was a wise man.

Did he feel the burden of his day lighten, lift when he saw a tiny
  sliver of time
Widen into possibility, solidify into reality, as, work done early,
His feet followed his heart into the woods
For a rare moment of solitude beneath shading trees at pond's edge
To name birds by their song, see the doe slake her thirst with
  dainty sips?
Left behind to find our own entertainment, we did not know we
  had given him
The gift of time, a gift of love.

Saturday Night Sashay

Bow to your partner—
   Before TV and after winter whist parties,
   Local and summer folks
   Met at Trail's End Hall to square-dance.
Bow to your corner—
   Long, low, polished wood floor,
   Windows open to warm nights,
   Narrow porch for cool-down, a bit of stargazing.
Heads forward and back—
   With General Patton precision and much humor,
   The caller called the sets.
   He was very good.
Sides forward and back—
   Music led the way, kept time.
   Feet fell in cadence.
   Trail's End pulsed.
Ladies star in—
   Hand of summer visitor slender,
   Soft, delicate, cluster of rings,
   Eyes warm, enjoying the fun, accepted.
All join hands—
   Middle-aged farmer's grip
   Callused from plow, haying, hoe,
   A reliable guide through the patterns, secure.
Do-si-do—
   Back to back with the boy
   The girl thought about all week.
   She ignored him—sort of.

The caller sang out—
    "Duck for the oyster, dig for the clam,
    Now through the hole in the old tin can."
    Only those in the know knew.
Swing your partner—
    The hall was a kaleidoscope.
    Skirts twirled, colors swirled,
    Rhythm kept, form preserved.
All promenade home—
    "Good night, Ladies, good night, Ladies.
    Until next week."
A grand time was had by all.

Vacationland July

I'm staying home today.
I've run out of hurry up,
Hit the floor, hit the shower, hit the road.
Time to hit the brakes

And taste each blueberry in the cereal bowl,
Savor scents on morning breezes,
Notice fleecy clouds fluffed in azure skies,
Deadhead the patio pansies in my PJs,
Chuckle at the feisty red squirrel
Dashing about, the biggest bully at the feeder,

Sip a cup of coffee slowly,
Declare this "fend for yourself" lunch day,
Drift into dreamless slumber at 3:10 p.m.,
Write a poetic line or two
Before the words fly off somewhere—
Gone forever,

Watch a stunning sunset fade into dusk,
Linger in a porch rocker, share a hushed conversation,
Count fireflies,
Then raise the windows wide, lights out,
Ending a lovely at-home vacation day.

Backward Glance
For Grandson Andrew, age 15

As your voice deepens into manhood,
My memory hears childhood glee.
I sat atop your bed-boat,
Read aloud adventures unlimited
While you, my brave Protector,
Donned eye patch and canteen,
Swashbuckled forth, sword in hand,
Challenged jungles and raging rivers,
Slew alligators and dragons
Upon the bedroom floor.

Oh, it was a glorious romp!

And Then

This morning something is amiss
following the goodbye hug and kiss.
A final wave as the car crests the hill,
I return to the kitchen, so still.
The scent of cinnamon and orange-fragrant air
Lingers after the farewell feast celebrated there.

Yesterday's guest towels, perky on the rack,
Now hang limp, rather slack.
Grandma's quilt, full of family history
Remember that touch of mystery?
Lies silent in careful fold
Until next time and the story is retold.

Making plans for things to do,
Exploring old places, some new,
A little rain, mostly fair, good times, talks,
Noisy gatherings, quiet walks.
I find myself listening in empty spaces
For voices on their way to other places.

Somewhere

An inner place lives somewhere
Just beyond every day,

Barely past that gauzy haze,
A pulse, a whisper-soft beat

Kept by an unseen keeper
Known only to me.

Different, I will say,
Not a lazy place at all.

Free from hurry-worry,
The pace is mine to choose,

Skip from thought to thought
Or drift from reverie to adventure.

I cannot name the colors
Though I know their beauty well.

Kindness and ethics are this kingdom's coin.
Perfume called peace lies lightly on the air.

A special place, a holy place,
My place of daydreams.

My House of Belonging

Where is my house of belonging?

I wander inner landscapes
With pen, candle, music,
Any season, day or night,

Pick words like wild flowers
To make my heart song
Soar with eagles

Or let silent tears tell the story
Of my sorrow, my lament,
And it is all right.

Friend

I weep. You feel my tears.
I hunger. You nourish me with understanding.
I thirst. You ease me with compassion's cup.
I bleed. You bind my wounds with laughter.
I whimper. You uphold me with your strength.
I look into your eyes and see acceptance and friendship.
We stand together in silence and I am at peace.

Hey, Stupid

How disheartening in this year of 2011
And be a tax-paying American
To D.C. and Augusta.
I expect a fair and reasonable return.
Instead trust fades, dreams tarnish.

Bailed bank CEOs double dip.
Pharmaceutical and insurance companies
Try to control our living and dying.
Car makers weep for handouts.
Bloated oil companies plead
For tax breaks
So they can "Drill, baby, drill,"
While alternative energy possibilities
Are ridiculed.

Billions are wasted, scammed
While the middle class wanes.
Homeless children are hungry,
Yet agra-complexes
Are paid not to plant.
Political nest-feathers
Block much-needed jobs for upcoming campaign slogans.
Education declines.
And I can't buy a toothbrush made in the USA.

Hey, Stupid,
Don't notice watered-down tomato paste,
Shrinking toilet paper rolls,
Fewer ounces in foodstuffs,
Air whipped into ice cream,
Bigger indents on bottle bottoms,
And larger trailer trucks on our stressed roads.

Hey, Stupid,
How would you like living
In a third-world country
As a second-class citizen?

Are you talking to ME?

Rhyme Revisited

Twinkle, twinkle, Little Star,
Can you see from where you are?
Is the Golden Rule a sham?
Can the Lion love the Lamb?

Please Don't Feed the Animals

There are elephants in the living room,
Monkeys frolic on the stair,
A lion lurks by the sofa,
Some skunks stroll in. Beware.

Bats doze behind a door
Waiting for night to fall.
Unseen chameleons are everywhere,
And herded sheep hesitate...then stall.

Donkeys bray at windows,
Ducks in rows look neither left nor right,
Kangaroos run the courts,
Snakes in the grass slither out of sight.

There is no joy in this tragic D.C. zoo.
America's life is on the line.
It breaks my heart to cast my vote,
Yet witness democracy's decline.

Trading Up

I would exchange the state of the union
for peace of mind,
negative news for a contented heart,
universal hate for individual love,
personal gain for moral right,
religious rhetoric for The Golden Rule,
political power for ethical living,
corporate greed for being my brother's keeper,
need to be right for thoughtful justice,
pork-barrel legislation for education,
political spin for truth,
manipulation for trust in peoples' goodness.

Who will hear my words?
Don't tell me Utopia! Unrealistic! Pie in the sky!
If it is, I'll have a slice. A big one, thank you.

A. Mouse Story

The space seemed small at the base of the wall
Though A. Mouse family didn't need height to make it right.
They were smart from the start,
Crept out at night, explored by starlight,
Found this and that; a crust, a wool hat.
The crust was shared for dinner, the hat was a winner.
Not needed for the head, it became their snug little bed.
They sat at a lost thimble table, exercised on the TV cable.
Happy and content, they knew what it meant
By living in a hole in the wall and making it a home, after all.

The Giraffe—A Most Unusual Creature

On polished ebony hoofs, with burl-like knees,
Ridiculously slender legs extending to flanks
Upholstered in short-haired fabric of unique design,
She lowers herself with utmost care
At water's edge, bends her willowy neck
And siphons water through an esophagus straw
To ease her thirst, knowing that
Predators prowl, ready to pounce
At the merest suggestion of unsteadiness
As she demurely sips from the muddy river.

Atop the sinuous neck sits the head.
Sensitive nostrils and canine-like ears
Are part of her alarm system.
Two fur-covered horns rise above a brow with a bony lump.

Silky-soft lips close over a tongue
Of great ability and length and strength.
That mouth spends a lifetime
Stripping leaves from thorny trees. Remarkable.

She is a browser. Her dignified pace throughout life
Is deliberate, graceful, unhurried, nonaggressive,
Although she can be decisive, swift, and protective
In her world of survival of the fittest.

I don't know what she thinks
Behind that knobbed forehead.
Her dark luminous eyes with sweeping lashes
Seem to look on the world
With gentleness, compassion, knowing,
And just a hint of humor.

The Good Life

My foot lingers on sun-warmed carpet
And I think how lovely to be a cat:
Wear a fur coat, silky-soft,
Bring forth chest-deep rumbly purr-songs
In gratitude for gentle strokes,
Gaze on the world with ancient feline wisdom,
Bestow blessings with my sweeping plum-tail
Or send "watch out" signals with annoyed twitches,
Return to kittenhood to pursue a sleep-dazed housefly,
Give my perfect self a perfect preen,
Find a sunbeam for an afternoon catnap.

I would live with attitude.

Pachyderm

The elephant stands, a sturdy gray house
Atop four solid oak pilings,
Strong against storms and wild beasts.
Amber eyes are alert in her battering-ram head.
The world trembles when she stomps her boilerplate foot.
Yet, with that stevedore trunk, gently, ever so gently,
She nudges her baby to her tender, nourishing nipple.

Fast Forward

To see a moment of pure bliss,
Take note of a dog, head out the window,
Whizzing down the highway.
It doesn't get any better.

There are hairy English sheepdogs,
Dainty toy poodles,
And all the marvelous mixed mutts between,
Including pen-and-ink Snoopy in his cockpit.

Big-dog drool blowing away in speed-limit wind,
Backseats fur-encased from thumping tails,
Windows smudged with nose prints,
All the telltale signs of a happy pooch.

Our beloved little Lucy
Became a canine figurehead
As she took her place on the most
Forward inch of the boat bow,
Short beagle legs stiff
To steady her in her regal spot,
Silky tan ears rippled in the breeze,
Always woofed a deep-chested "land-ho"
As we neared the island.
She smiled her doggy smile.
Lovely to see.

Going faster than four legs.
Now that's a lucky, joyous dog.

Springtime Pantomime

On a March day of rainy dullness,
Canadas, sedate in formal suits of quill and down,
Blended with the dun of the winter marsh.
They moved with slow stately pace,
Heads to the ground in graceful arches
Except for the upright sentry on duty.

But wait. A flash!

Mallards, with shiny emerald feather hats,
Stumpy legs pumping up and down in bright orange galoshes,
Dashed among the geese.
They were circus clowns let loose in center ring,
Amusing, uplifting, celebrating spring.

Dinner with Friends

They eat seed and corn
When they dine at my house
And sip from a communal cup.

The multiple-choice menu
Is served dawn to dusk
With no variation year in, year out.

The Cardinal, in his flashy red suit,
Often brings the Mrs. along.
Sometimes the kids make it a party of four.

Jays, not intimidated by red,
Dazzle in blue and white,
Shout and argue all the time. All the time.

Ample-breasted Mourning Doves
Totter about on stumpy legs,
Fastidious, selective, muttering in hushed tones.

Chickadee sings *Chickadee-dee*;
Such a welcome song on white-quiet winter days,
Eats sunflower seed. Takes one home for later.

Turkey, magnificently iridescent,
Swoops and struts for his hen harem,
Scolds at my door if his dinner is late. Pompous.

Goldfinches come by for thistle-seed dessert.
Jubilant Red-Winged Blackbirds announce spring.
There are Warblers and Sparrows. Some stay. Some pass through.

Gray Squirrels play tag, munch peanuts
While the Chipmunk stuffs his cheeks
With corn to hoard under the tool shed.

Later I will carry a tray
To the shaded back porch
And enjoy a delightful dinner with friends.

After the Blizzard

The dancing snow spirals horizon high
To fall once more from the sky,
Or wisps across the frozen field
Until it meets a rock that will not yield
And piles the drifts deeper yet.
As day draws down, the sun breaks through to set
With purple shadows and golden hue
 Under a patch of softest blue.
This stormy day's brief benediction is a sigh
In pastel lavender before night's waking eye.
With steady course, the moon will sail
Her indigo arc, pouring pale
Illumination on winter white here below,
This breathtaking, beautiful world of snow.

Slow Motion

The stone, heavy,
Unyielding except for
Tides and glacial shifts,
Sat solid.

But wait. A tulip bulb,
Pulled from winter slumber
By an insistent April sun,
Sent out a pointed bud

Through chilly loam
Beneath the stone,
Pushed upward
Toward promised Spring,

Unfolded its blaze of glory
And preformed a dance of passion
In gaudy ritual
For the sweet-starved bee.

The tulip had inched the stone aside
An unseen millimeter.
Nature settled herself,
And life, as always, moved on.

Change

September breezes blow
Dog days off center stage.
Gardens relax their labor,
Weary roses release final petals.
Tomatoes, rich with sweetness,
Warm in morning sun.

Noontime heat scatters before a cold front
With psychedelic light-show flashes
And drum rolls of thunder.
Pulsating rain pounds to keep the beat.

Later, strains of season's requiem
Fade across calming skies
As early evening's golden glow
Edges through passing clouds
To ignite a tiny maple leaf...
The first red flame of fall.
Summer sighs goodbye.

Disgruntled

I'm mad at Spring this year,
The lazy slug-a-bed.
Late in March I whispered, "Good morning."
It dumped a blizzard on my head.

It snuggled deeper under drifted cover
As wind blew cold from the north.
"It's April, it's April," I said,
"Pussy willows want to venture forth."

"Wake up. Time to be awake."
"Ho-hum," was the chilly reply.
The fog rolled in to stay a while
Beneath a misty, steely sky.

"Where is Spring?" I cried in May.
Wrathful wind tore tulip petals apart.
Lilac's perfume smelled of watered cologne,
And where was the blooming bleeding heart?

The seeds are rotted in the ground.
Spring turned its back on farmers' pleas.
Bees had nary a nectar sip.
It's now too late for early lettuce, tomatoes, peas.

"Will we ever see the sun again?"
Was my moldy moan on the first of June.
Got my wish. It reached 90 in the shade.
Spring was skipped and Summer came too soon.

Winter's Coming

Winter's coming. Make it slow.
It's too soon for Christmas lights, icy snow,
Furry boots, gloves to lose,
Soft and wooly scarves to choose,
Turtlenecks or mocks
To match long cozy socks.

New Year horns nor Valentine capers
Make up for windshield scrapers.
There's no time to take it easy
When drafts on ankles feel so breezy.
I'll huddle in quilts, there to stay
'til the calendar says April or May.
Winter's coming. Make it slow.

Sunset Symphony

Golden afternoon's glow,
tune up for sunset symphonies
with pearl-gray oboes,
soft blue French horns,
neon-orange cymbals, lilac violins,
fill the sky with all the drama that's bearable,
stays just long enough,
then steals away at horizon's edge.
In the gloaming
a star whispers flute notes
of serenity that is nightfall's lullaby.

A Matter of Perspective

I look in the mirror and see
An aging face reflected back at me
With lines that are here to stay
Beyond the remedy of creams night and day.
Yet with a smile they fall into place,
Smoothing away a wrinkly face.
I don't peer through glasses that are bi-focal,
Keeping the glance general, not specifically local.
I've earned this face that is mine for life,
Shaped by ups and downs, laughter and strife.
With passing years, here is the conclusion:
Content counts, the container's illusion.

Purple Funk

My fire is full of irons.
My teapot is full of tempest.
My ointment is full of flies.
My head is full of steam.
My house needs downsizing.
My wardrobe needs upgrading.
I have been politically incorrect,
A day late and a dollar short.
I have burned bridges and the midnight oil.
Headlines in last week's paper:
"People do die of broken hearts."
No news to me. I've known it for decades.
I have passed several ships in the night.
Some days hope goes galley-west.
Some days dreams don't amount to diddly-squat.
It's easy to forget to grow old with grace.
Time stands still but waits for no one.
Gung ho! Let's go. Let's go.

I need a vacation.

If I Lived in Nebraska

If I lived in Nebraska, would the wind sing to me
As does the surf on sand and shore;
Would waves of wheat move me
As the tides of the mighty Atlantic;
Would crow's caw tell me a story
As does the gull's raucous cry;
Would prairie breeze flavor my lips
As does the touch of ocean's salty fog;
Would distant fading day offer up
Heart-stopping, breathtaking sunsets;
Would vast nighttime skies comfort
As do New England's gentle, forested hills?

Who would I be in a land named Nebraska?

2 A.M. Post-Op, Post-Op

I'm so tired of thinking of me.
Pills, pain, to ice or not the knee,
Exercise, massage, try for the best,
Get settled for a while. Then there is the breast
That had a lump, lurking and growing,
A threat to life without my knowing.
The surgeon did his work well,
Wide margins, clear nodes, as far as he can tell.
There is a new doctor to take my case;
Radiologist-oncologist, a name, unknown face,
Already had the data to shape my fate,
Settle the questions, "Soon enough? Not too late?"
Things could be worse in every way
Yet I feel off-center from my everyday.
This body is a muddle, taking emotions along.
One moment it's weepy, next hums a song.
Life has dealt a double slam,
Right now I don't know exactly who I am.

Freedom

I flew away in a big metal bird
To an ancient land of old and new
Where I was at home.
Spring, blessed spring, was in the air,
Celebrated by removing the liner of my coat
With a liberating, gleeful zip.

Descending the Tube stairway to heaven,
Breezes from the rushing trains
Stirred my hair
As a saxophonist with upturned hat at his feet
Gave me a wonderful-world Satchmo gift.

Long walks across the park
To catch the Big Red Bus
Offered up budded daffodils
That bloomed golden by week's end.
Broad sidewalks beckoned.

Young ladies in short, lace-trimmed dresses
And colorful tailored coats
Tapped along on straw-thin stilettos.
The men, at ease in their business suits
With coordinated shirts and ties
Were...spiffy, handsome.

Daytime and evenings of delight,
Plays, people, pubs,
Bustling streets, Harrods,
Quiet spaces, open-air markets
Where treasures waited for me...

This is my love song to London
That I will hum for a long, long time.

Echo

Once more I weep silent tears
That echo down solitary years
To that quiet shaded bower
Where we shared a precious hour
Of harmony in thought and song.
The sad world entered in, the tune was gone.
Love, on satin tiptoes, slipped away
Except in my heart, for it would stay
In that undimmed place of youth
Where dreams meld with truth
To make us who we are today...
World apart, but never far away.

What?

I might miss the wonder of wonderful,
The giddy gasp of glee,
The dazzle of delight,
The thrill of transcendency,
The razzamatazz of rapture,
The sigh of serenity.
It's *huh?* Instead of *aha!*

There are times I just don't get it.

Thursday

Thirty-seven-plus years of tucking away
For later use, might need, special gifts,
Holders of family history in things.

Tiny hand prints in plaster,
Valentines of faded red and crumpled lace,
Blankets soft with wear and memories,
Linens last folded by beloved hands now still,
Art created in clay, paint, wood, and wool,
China cups, books, something for everyone.

I shall not sigh sorting through
Or pause by the boxes and heaps.
I will strive for the goal,
The lightness of peeling away,
Think of a job well done.

I must make a sign—YARD SALE!

Grumble, Grumble

I come from the
Tap, jostle, thump, shake,
Bobby pin, nail file
School of repair.

This puts me out of step,
Way out of step and into deep water
With the foisted-on-me
Techno, high-speed age of
Plugging into the whole world
Via mouse and lingo from
Palm-held to laptop.

They tell me, "You've come a long way, baby."

Spam used to be something
My aunt chopped, added some relish, Miracle Whip,
Spread between two pieces of bread
And always brought to every family picnic.
Everybody liked those sandwiches.

Big Hand on Six

It's always half-past something:

Half-past nine—edging toward late,

Half-past summer—red, white, and blue rockets blaze,

Half-past motherhood—two silent bedrooms,

Half-past robust—pills, patch, replace,

Half-past marriage—silver and gold,

Half-past cherished ones—circles broken.

Yet it's only half.

May my life be full

Until the big hand is on twelve.

Query

That familiar face,
Known since childhood,
Unchanged.

It's always something...
Fast, slow, hurry up,
Soon, late, early, wasted,
Too much, never enough.

Hands never still,
Moving, moving.
Fancy or plain,
Uninvolved, remote,
A ticking yardstick.

Who invented clocks?

Star Wish

I rue the nights sans slumber,
Counting worries without number.
How do they know day is done,
Start to stir at setting sun,
Nibble at the edge of sleep
Then make a quantum leap
To thunder through my head,
Rob me of a restful bed?

I long to linger with Fishermen Three
In Nod where dreams are free,
With silver nets, ocean sky,
And the moon winks as we sail by.

A Piece of Marble

Who is in that rock?
Someone harsh and heavy,
Carrying the world's unbearable weight,
Pushing away, overpowering?

Or someone light and lovely,
Enticing the eye,
Flowing lines reaching to embrace
A world needing comfort?

Is there a choice?
Does the artist move close
With hand and soul to create,
Or does the stone demand its life?

Sizing Up

Big things break my heart.
Little things make my day.
The heartbreak list needs no length.
It overwhelms with tenacity and strength.
Disease beyond medical or spiritual reach,
False religions that preach
That all men are not brothers,
Justifies destruction and killing others,
Plant and nurture the hate seed
For political gain and personal greed,
View the female gender with disdain,
Disregard freedom, loss, and pain,
Destroy cultures, create war,
Practice cruelty, ignore law,
Take, beat, maim for power
Marching down the ages hour by hour.
Hear, oh Man, the do-unto-others Golden Rule.
And yet...
It may seem a little thing
When a friend answers on second ring,
Supper's ready in a savory pot
Of stew, biscuit-crowned—the golden sort,
A lad, of almost seven-and-a-half,
Honors my knock-knock joke with a laugh,
A babe with drool on its chin
Gives the world a toothless grin,
A bit of solitude amid the fray
Bestows renewal along the way.
These moments of ordinary pleasure
Are my small but priceless treasure.
One on one, two then four,
Hand in hand, reach for more.
Hope.

Let Me

Let me live with a lusty laugh,
The real thing, nothing by half,
No jeers, no scorn, no lukewarm tee-hee.
Let me gasp for breath, slap my knee.

May endorphins dance to scatter fears,
Ease my heart past midnight tears,
Mend the horrors made by man.
See the better side when I can

And know the humor in the human race,
Give the funny-bone its honored place,
Fan the flame of hope, feel the spirit lift,
Freely share a smile...such a tiny gift

In the empty day of a lonely stranger
Or child trying to love a world in danger
Of sinking under the weight of gloom.
Choices and chances pass in a plume

Of yesterday's illusions as wispy as air.
May laughter lighten my load of care
And the damp on my cheek be from joy or glee.
Let me laugh for pleasure, slap my knee.